T0083333

Nikki Iles

Violin

Jazz in Autumn

9 pieces for violin and piano

Contents

	Page
(Somewhere) Over the Rainbow	3
Hay Barn Blues	4
Autumn Leaves	6
Des Vendanges	8
Here's That Rainy Day	9
Danny Boy	11
Harvest Calypso	12
September in the Rain	14
Gypsy Waltz	16

CD track information is given at the top of each piece, in the form **1**, 12, with the first (bold) number indicating the full performance track, and the second number the piano-only backing track.

MUSIC DEPARTMENT

OXFORD
UNIVERSITY PRESS

Arranger's note

I was delighted to be asked to continue this seasonal series for violin and piano and to have the pleasure of recording, once again, with the wonderful Ros Stephen. I am also grateful to Margrit Hasler for her invaluable contribution in the early stages of writing these pieces. Researching the various violinists who have shaped each genre has been enlightening for me and helped to bring a broad stylistic base to the collection on this theme of autumn.

The book takes you through a variety of musical styles from the Blue Grass of 'Hay Barn Blues' to the Cuban 'Des Vendanges' (grape harvest); and from the joyous swing of 'Autumn Leaves' to the rich harmonies of jazz classics such as '(Somewhere) Over The Rainbow' and 'Here's That Rainy Day'. The accompanying CD is provided to help you with the interpretation of the various styles—specifically the 'feel' of each piece. You will notice that Ros paraphrases the melody on the second time around the tune in 'Autumn Leaves' and also adds a few of her own 'slides' in 'Hay Barn Blues'. The notation here is just the starting point, so please, please feel free to interpret these arrangements in your own way!

OXFORD
UNIVERSITY PRESS

Great Clarendon Street, Oxford OX2 6DP,
United Kingdom

Oxford University Press is a department of the University of Oxford.
It furthers the University's aim of excellence in research, scholarship,
and education by publishing worldwide. Oxford is a registered trade mark of
Oxford University Press in the UK and in certain other countries

This collection © Oxford University Press 2016

Nikki Iles has asserted her right under the Copyright, Designs
and Patents Act, 1988, to be identified as the Author of these Works

First published 2016

Impression: 6

All rights reserved. No part of this publication may be reproduced,
stored in a retrieval system, or transmitted, in any form or by any means,
without the prior permission in writing of Oxford University Press

Permission to perform the works in this anthology in public
(except in the course of divine worship) should normally be obtained
from a local performing right licensing organization, unless the owner
or the occupier of the premises being used already holds a licence
from such an organization. Likewise, permission to make and exploit a
recording of these works should be obtained from a local mechanical
copyright licensing organization

Enquiries concerning reproduction outside the scope of the above should
be directed to the Music Rights Department, Oxford University Press,
at music.permissions.uk@oup.com or at the address above

ISBN 978-0-19-340767-1

Music origination by Katie Johnson

Printed in Great Britain on acid-free paper by
Halstan & Co. Ltd, Amersham, Bucks.

Credits
Cover illustration by Tony Stephenson © Oxford University Press
Artist photo by Hugh Byrne

The *Violin Jazz in Autumn* CD was recorded at Red Gables Facilities,
Greenford, on 28 April 2016. Engineered, co-produced, and edited
by Ken Blair, BMP The Sound Recording Company Ltd.

(Somewhere) Over the Rainbow

words by E. Y. HARBURG
music by HAROLD ARLEN
arr. Nikki Iles

inspired by Mark Feldman

© 1938 Metro-Goldwyn-Mayer Inc., EMI Feist Catalog Inc. EMI United Partnership Limited. All rights reserved. International copyright secured. Used by permission of Alfred Music Publishing Co. and Music Sales Group. Photocopying this copyright material is ILLEGAL.

tracks **2**, 11

Hay Barn Blues

NIKKI ILES

© Oxford University Press 2016. Photocopying this copyright material is ILLEGAL.

inspired by Big Bill Broonzy

tracks **3**, 12

Autumn Leaves

words by JACQUES PRÉVERT
music by JOSEPH KOSMA
arr. Nikki Iles

© 1947 Peter Maurice Music Co. Ltd. This arrangement © 2016 Peter Maurice Music Co. Ltd. All rights reserved. International Copyright Secured. Used by permission of Alfred Music Publishing Co. and Music Sales Group. Photocopying this copyright material is ILLEGAL.

inspired by Didier Lockwood

tracks 4,13

Des Vendanges

NIKKI ILES

© Oxford University Press 2016. Photocopying this copyright material is ILLEGAL.

Nikki Iles

Violin

Jazz in Autumn

Piano accompaniment book

Contents

	Page
(Somewhere) Over the Rainbow	2
Hay Barn Blues	6
Autumn Leaves	10
Des Vendanges	15
Here's That Rainy Day	20
Danny Boy	25
Harvest Calypso	28
September in the Rain	31
Gypsy Waltz	36

MUSIC DEPARTMENT

OXFORD
UNIVERSITY PRESS

(Somewhere) Over the Rainbow

words by E. Y. HARBURG
music by HAROLD ARLEN
arr. Nikki Iles

© 1938 Metro-Goldwyn-Mayer Inc., EMI Feist Catalog Inc. EMI United Partnership Limited. All rights reserved. International copyright secured. Used by permission of Alfred Music Publishing Co. and Music Sales Group. Photocopying this copyright material is ILLEGAL.

Expressively ♩ = 60
9
mp
3
12
15
mp
2
mp
18
mf
1
mf

21
mp
mp
24
p
p
Ped.
Ped.
27
mp
mp
p
p cresc.
mp cresc.
30
mf
mf

inspired by Mark Feldman

Hay Barn Blues

NIKKI ILES

© Oxford University Press 2016. Photocopying this copyright material is ILLEGAL.

10
mf
f
mf
f
Ped.
13
mf
mf
17
f
f
20
mf
mf

23
mp
27
pizz.
mf
arco
pizz.
31
arco
mf
mf
35
pizz.
arco
mp
f
mp

inspired by Big Bill Broonzy

Autumn Leaves

words by JACQUES PRÉVERT
music by JOSEPH KOSMA
arr. Nikki Iles

© 1947 Peter Maurice Music Co. Ltd. This arrangement © 2016 Peter Maurice Music Co. Ltd. All rights reserved. International Copyright Secured. Used by permission of Alfred Music Publishing Co. and Music Sales Group. Photocopying this copyright material is ILLEGAL.

10
mp
sim.
14
mf
mf
18
mf
mf
to Coda
22
mp
mp

26
mf
mf
mp
29
mf
32
mp
mp
35
mf
f
mf
f

39
42
mf
mf
46
mf
50
f
f

inspired by Didier Lockwood

Des Vendanges

NIKKI ILES

© Oxford University Press 2016. Photocopying this copyright material is ILLEGAL.

12
mf
mf
slightly pull back
a tempo
15
mp
mf
mp
18
mf
mf
22
mf
mp
mf

26
p
mf
mp
mp
30
mp
mf
Ped.
34
mf
mp
p
38
mp
mf

42
pizz.
mf
f
46
A little faster
mf
50
arco
mf
54
mp

inspired by Omar Puente

Here's That Rainy Day

words by JOHNNY BURKE
music by JIMMY VAN HEUSEN
arr. Nikki Iles

© 1953 Burke-Van-Heusen Inc. and Dorsey Brothers Music Inc., USA, Marke Music Publishing Co., Inc., Spirit Two Music, Inc., Van Heusen Music Corp., Onyx Music Corp., Chester Music Ltd trading as Campbell Connelly & Co., and Bourne Co. All rights for Marke Music Publishing Co., Inc. administered by WB Music Corp. Copyright renewed. All rights reserved. International copyright secured. Used by permission of Faber Music Ltd, Alfred Music Publishing Co., Music Sales Ltd, and Bourne Music Publishing Co. Photocopying this copyright material is ILLEGAL.

13
mp
mf
mp
mf
17
mf
Ped.
21
mf
25
Intensely
mp
mf
mp
mf

29
mp
mf
mp
mf
3
Broadly
rall.
33
f
3
2
3
mp
f
mp
a tempo
37
mf
mp
mf
41
mf
mp
mp
mf

45
mp
mf
49
mf
mp
mp
53
mf
mf
opt. 8va (until b. 63)
57
f
f
mf
mf
Ped.

inspired by Chris Garrick

Danny Boy

trad. Irish
arr. Nikki Iles

© Oxford University Press 2014 and 2016. Photocopying this copyright material is ILLEGAL.

13
mp
mf
mf
mp
mf
16
rall.
a tempo
rall.
mp
mp
p
p
19
Ballad (in time) ♩ = 52
mp
mp
mf
mf
22
mf
mf

inspired by Yehudi Menuhin

Harvest Calypso

NIKKI ILES

© Oxford University Press 2014 and 2016. Photocopying this copyright material is ILLEGAL.

14
1.
2.
mf
mf
mf
17
mf
21
f
to Coda
1.
2.
mf
mf
mf
mp
mp
25
mf
mp
mf

inspired by Regina Carter

September in the Rain

words by AL DUBIN
music by HARRY WARREN
arr. Nikki Iles

© 1937 WB Music Corp. Warner/Chappell North America Ltd., London, W8 5DA. Reproduced by permission of Faber Music Ltd. All rights reserved. Photocopying this copyright material is ILLEGAL.

12
mf
mf
15
mp
mp
mf
18
mf
21
mf
mf

25
f
f
29
mp
mp
33
to Coda
mf
mf
mf
mf
1
3
37
3

40
mf
mf
43
f
mp
f
mp
46
mf
mp
mf
50
mf
mf
mf
D.S. al Coda

inspired by the George Shearing Quintet

Gypsy Waltz

trad.
arr. Nikki Iles

© Oxford University Press 2016. Photocopying this copyright material is ILLEGAL.

15
mf
mf
19
opt. 8va (until b. 24)
(1)
(2)
23
mp
mp
mf
28
mf
mp

inspired by Stéphane Grappelli

inspired by Omar Puente

tracks **5**, 14

Here's That Rainy Day

words by JOHNNY BURKE
music by JIMMY VAN HEUSEN
arr. Nikki Iles

Gentle, understated bossa nova ♩ = 108

V. S.

© 1953 Burke-Van-Heusen Inc. and Dorsey Brothers Music Inc., USA, Marke Music Publishing Co., Inc., Spirit Two Music, Inc., Van Heusen Music Corp., Onyx Music Corp., Chester Music Ltd trading as Campbell Connelly & Co., and Bourne Co. All rights for Marke Music Publishing Co., Inc. administered by WB Music Corp. Copyright renewed. All rights reserved. International copyright secured. Used by permission of Faber Music Ltd, Alfred Music Publishing Co., Music Sales Ltd, and Bourne Music Publishing Co. Photocopying this copyright material is ILLEGAL.

inspired by Chris Garrick

Danny Boy

trad. Irish
arr. Nikki Iles

© Oxford University Press 2014 and 2016. Photocopying this copyright material is ILLEGAL.

tracks **7**, 16

Harvest Calypso

NIKKI ILES

© Oxford University Press 2014 and 2016. Photocopying this copyright material is ILLEGAL.

inspired by Regina Carter

tracks **8**, 17

September in the Rain

words by AL DUBIN
music by HARRY WARREN
arr. Nikki Iles

© 1937 WB Music Corp. Warner/Chappell North America Ltd., London, W8 5DA. Reproduced by permission of Faber Music Ltd. All rights reserved. Photocopying this copyright material is ILLEGAL.

inspired by the George Shearing Quintet

tracks **9**, 18

Gypsy Waltz

trad.
arr. Nikki Iles

inspired by Stéphane Grappelli

© Oxford University Press 2016. Photocopying this copyright material is ILLEGAL.